Talking Drums of Africa

Talking Drums of Africa

by
CHRISTINE PRICE

CHARLES SCRIBNER'S SONS
NEW YORK [C 1973]

Author's Note

The poems quoted in this book are from the following sources:

The two extracts from Yoruba praise poems are taken from *Yoruba Poetry: Traditional Yoruba Poems,* collected and translated by Bakare Gbadamosi and Ulli Beier. Special Publication of *Black Orpheus,* Ibadan, 1959.

The Ashanti poems are taken from translations of drum poetry made by J. H. K. Nketia. I am most grateful to Professor Nketia for his permission to use these quotations and also for his help and encouragement during my visit to Ghana.

I would like to thank all those who helped along the way in West Africa, and especially the drummers and the dancers who fired me with enthusiasm for their art.

1 3 5 7 9 11 13 15 17 19 RD/C 20 18 16 14 12 10 8 6 4 2
Printed in the United States of America
Library of Congress Catalog Card Number 73-6405
SBN 684-13492-6 (cloth)

**This book is for RACHEL
who loves to dance**

DRUMS!

    DRUMS!

     DRUMS!

Who has not heard of African drums?

**The peoples of Africa make music
on many kinds of instruments,
but north, south, east and west
you will hear the beat of drums.**

You hear the drums in cities,

in villages,

and in the palaces of African kings.

You hear them at festivals

and funerals

and joyful times of worship, prayer and praise.

As you listen to their rhythm,
you can feel the drums,
beating in your body,
in your hands and your feet,
telling you to move,
telling you to dance.

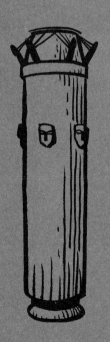

But African drums can do more.

The drums speak.

The drums sing.

The drums have stories to tell.

There are many parts of Africa
where people play talking drums.
The countries of western Africa
are famous for drums and drummers.
In Nigeria and Ghana
we can hear whole orchestras of drums
that build up great patterns of rhythm
and boom with a thundering sound.
These are the lands we shall go to
in search of talking drums.

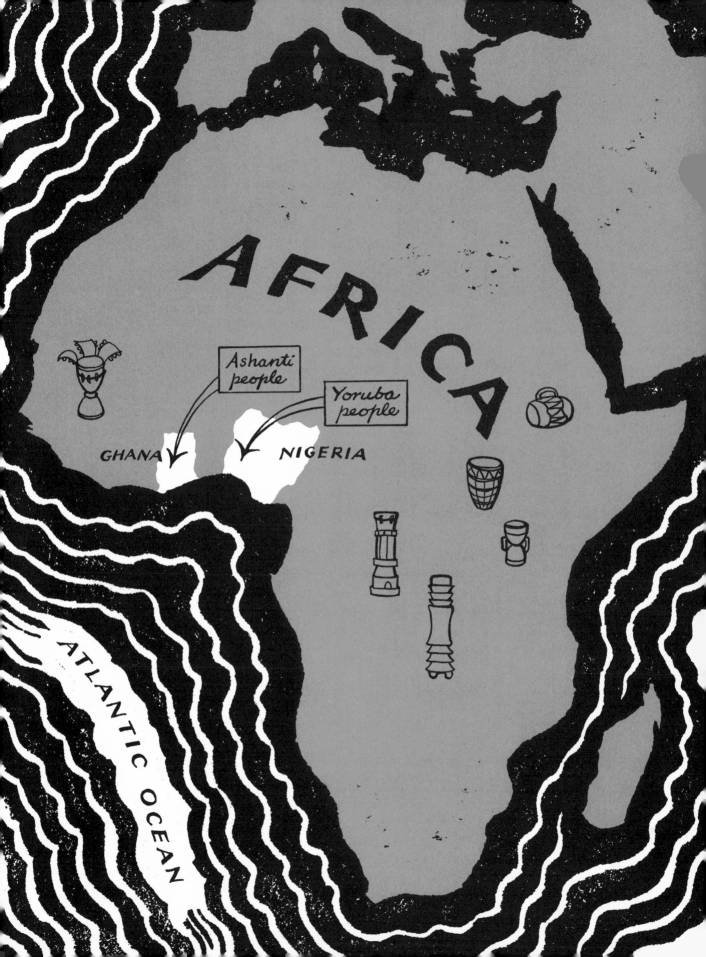

AFRICA

Ashanti
people

Yoruba
people

GHANA   NIGERIA

ATLANTIC OCEAN

In NIGERIA we shall make our way
to the land of the Yoruba people.
We are lucky and come to a Yoruba town
on a day of celebration,
when the king of the town comes out of his palace
with a big procession.
The streets are full of people,
dressed in their finest clothes,
and somewhere, far away,
we can hear the sound of drums.

Louder and louder the drums are beating,

and now, look there!

    Stand out of the way!

The procession comes!

The royal procession with the palace drums!

Here they come dancing
through the middle of the town—
the king up ahead and his drummers behind him,
beating on their <u>dundun</u> drums,
beating out his praises on their drums.
The Master Drummer has the leading drum
with bells around the drumhead
that shiver and jingle.

That is IYA ILU, the great Mother Drum,
and behind is KANANGO, the smallest drum,
played by the smallest of the drummers.

The <u>dundun</u> drums are like a family,

and each one has a name.

After IYA ILU and tiny KANANGO

there are KERIKERI,

GANGAN,

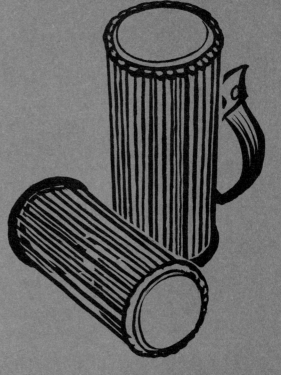

and the little round drum
that is called GUDUGUDU.

All of the drums, except the little round one,
have a long wooden body with bowl-shaped ends
and a slender waist in the middle.
The ends are covered
with goatskin drumheads,
laced together with thongs or cords,
stretched down the length
of the drum.

If you watch the Master Drummer

as he passes by,

you can see how he presses

on the cords of his drum.

Pressing on the cords

will tighten the drumheads,

and the sound of the drum

will be sharp and high.

When he slackens his hold

and the drumheads loosen,

the notes he strikes are low.

He can play many notes

on his <u>dundun</u> drum.

His drum can talk and sing!

IYA ILU, KERIKERI,

   GANGAN and KANANGO—

all of them are talking drums.

With their high and low notes

they can mimic the sound

of words in the Yoruba language.

In English you can say "Hello" or "How are you?"

as high or as low as you like.

In the language of the Yoruba people,

and in other African tongues,

each word has its proper note.

Sentences in Yoruba go up and down
like the music of a song,
and the same word, spoken on different notes,
can have quite different meanings.
<u>Ilu</u> (on two low notes) means "drum";
   but <u>Ilu</u> (low-high) means "town";
      and <u>Ilu</u> (low-middle) means "gimlet."

A <u>dundun</u> drummer can match so well
the notes and rhythms of speaking
that people can hear every word that he says
in the language of the drum.

The royal drummers can spread good news

or warn the people of danger.

When someone important arrives at the palace,

the drummers announce his coming.

They must know how to play his own special praise-song

that tells of his wealth or his courage in war.

Great kings are greeted with splendid songs:

> Child of death,
>
> Father of all mothers,
>
> King of all kings.
>
> You carry the blackness of the forest
>
> like a royal gown.
>
> You carry the blood of your enemies
>
> like a shining crown....

And the drummers praise the gods
of the Yoruba people,
in songs like this one for the kindly god
who made all human beings:

He is patient, he is not angry.

He sits in silence to pass judgment.

He sees you even when he is not looking.

He stays in a far place—

but his eyes are on the town.

He stays by his children and lets them succeed.

He causes them to laugh — and they laugh.

Ohoho — the father of laughter.

His eye is full of joy.

He rests in the sky like a swarm of bees.

We dance to our sixteen drums that sound jingin, jingin,

To eight of the drums we dance bending down,

To eight of the drums we dance erect.

We shake our shoulders, we shake our hips,

Munusi, munusi, munusi,

We dance to your sixteen drums....

The drums talk,

the drums sing,

and <u>dundun</u> drummers play for everyone —

not just for kings.

Down to the market goes a drummer with his son,

a little boy learning how to drum.

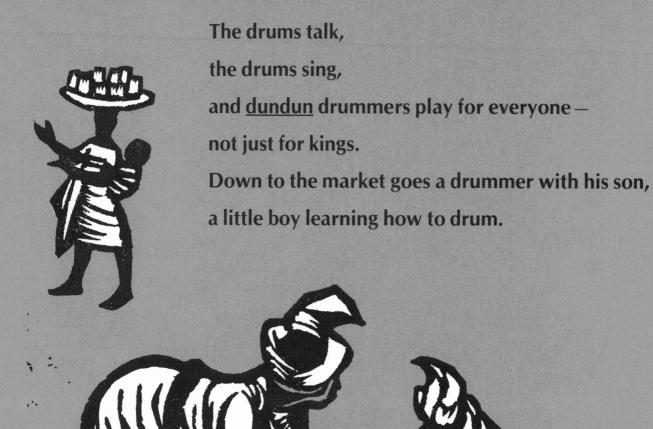

They are playing praise-songs for the market women,
and each woman smiles and gives them money,
happy to be told by the <u>dundun</u> drums
she is beautiful and wise!

In GHANA too is a talking drum,

a drum like the <u>dundun</u> — its name is <u>donno</u>.

But there we shall hear much bigger drums,

the deep-toned voices of <u>fontomfrom</u>

and the talking drums of the Ashanti.

When we go north from the city of Accra,

through the land of the Ashanti people,

we pass tall forests along the road

with tree trunks big enough to make big drums.

When a chief of Ashanti needs talking drums —

and only a ruler may own them —

the drum-maker goes to the forest

and finds a cedar tree.

He breaks an egg on the tree trunk

as an offering to the tree,

and he asks the tree for leave to cut it down

and carve <u>atumpan</u> drums.

The wood of one cedar will make many drums.

The drum-maker cuts out the bodies of two,

and shapes and hollows them.

The drumheads are leather from an elephant's ear,

fastened down on the top of each drum

with cords and wooden pegs.

The last thing to carve
on the pair of drums
is the small square "eye"
that will face the drummer,
the high chief's drummer
who will play the drums
on the day of the festival.

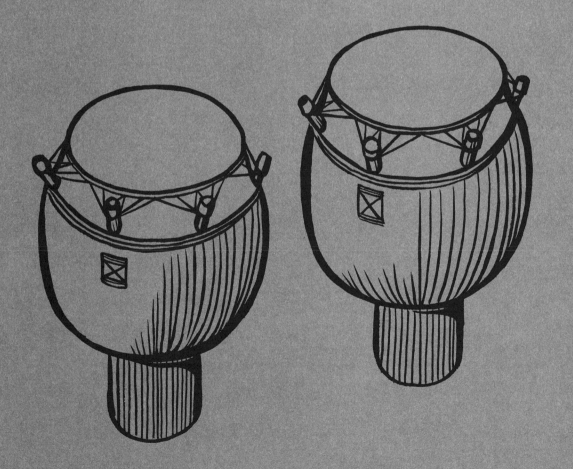

On that great day the drumming begins

long before the rising of the sun.

In the palace of the chief the drummer is alone,

his new drums tuned and ready to play.

The drum on his right will speak high like a woman;

the one on the left will sound low like a man.

Between them the two <u>atumpan</u> drums

will be able to speak in Ashanti language,

copying the music of spoken words,

the words that are spoken high or low.

The drummer takes his drumsticks and begins to talk

in the voices of the drums:

      Opoku the Fair One, I have bestirred myself.

      I am about to play on the talking drums.

      Talking drums, if you have been away,

      I am calling you; they say come.

      I am learning; let me succeed.

Then the drummer speaks to all the things
that went into the making of his drums:

Wood of the drum, Tweneboa Akwa...
Cedar wood, if you have been away,
I am calling you; they say come.
I am learning; let me succeed.

He speaks to the trumpeting elephant
whose ear was made into drumheads:

Elephant, Kotomirefi, that frees Kotoko,

Elephant of Kotoko that swallows other elephants...

Shall we go forward? We shall find men fighting.

Shall we press on? We shall find men fleeing.

Let us go forward in great haste,

Treading the path beaten by the Elephant,

The Elephant that shatters the axe,

The monstrous one, unmindful of bullets....

He greets the wide earth under his feet:

Earth when I am about to die, I depend on you.

When I am in life, I depend on you.

Earth that receives the body of the dead,

Good morning to you, Earth. Good morning, Great One.

I am learning; let me succeed.

And he speaks to the cock that crows for day:

When I was going to bed, I was not sleepy.

When I felt like sleeping, my eyes never closed.

All night he stood in his coop,

While children lay in bed asleep.

Early in the morning he was hailed:

"Good morning to you, Mr. Cock!"

The cock crows in the morning,

The cock rises to crow before the crack of dawn.

I am learning; let me succeed.

At daylight the drummer awakes the chief,

for today the chief will remember and honor

the souls of his ancestors,

the warrior chiefs who ruled the town

in ancient days of war.

Those were the times when the talking drums

would call out the people to fight,

and the summons was drummed

from village to village

across the land of Ashanti.

Today the people are flocking to town
to honor their chief, to give him greetings,
to dance, to sing and to hear the drums.
On the edge of the town in the morning heat
we can hear the drums from far away.
They lead us on to the palace gate —
the throbbing and booming of <u>fontomfrom</u>,
the great drum orchestra!

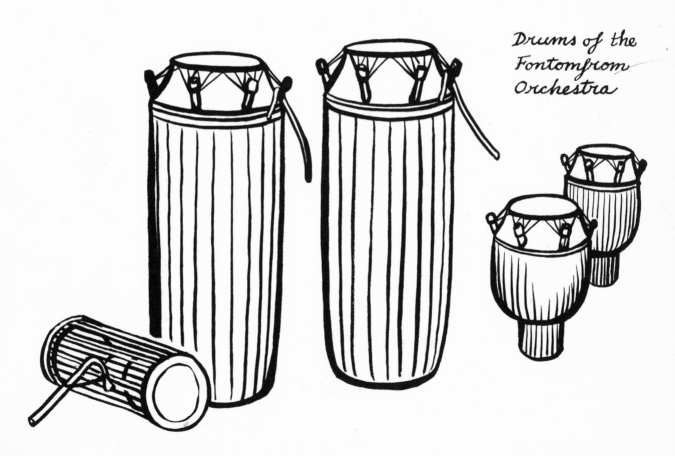

Drums of the
Fontomfrom
Orchestra

What a sight it is outside the palace!

Hundreds of people are gathered there

to see the chief enthroned in state

in a glitter of silk and gold,

and to watch the dancers, one by one,

come out to dance to the drums.

We see the drummer with his talking drums

standing behind the chief.

He plays for the dance with all the rest,

but then the drumming stops.

The dancer is gone.

Is the dancing done?

A hush has come, and the people listen,

and then we hear the talking drums,

speaking in words that are old and wise

about everlasting things:

The path has crossed the river,

The river has crossed the path,

Which is the elder?

We made the path and found the river,

The river is from long ago,

From the Creator of the Universe.

And now with a roar the drums join in —

the thundering voices of <u>fontomfrom</u> —

to take up the rhythm,

the rhythm of the words,

the message of the talking drums.

The dancer springs into the dancing ring,

and the beat of the words

that are old and wise

is the rhythm of his dance,

a warrior's dance of strength and skill,

a dance of victory.

Drums, drums, drums!

The booming voices of drums!

The drums speak,

the drums sing,

the drums have stories to tell.

Wherever the talking drums are heard

in the lands of Africa,

the sound of their voice is as new as today,

and older than anyone knows.

Long before stories were written down,

they were told on the talking drums.

The men of the past who were wise and strong

Come alive in the throb of the drums.

The people who listen are proud to hear,

and the drummers are filled with pride.

And Ashanti drummers will say,

in the language of the drums,

that when the world was made

a Drummer was first to come

from the Great Creator's hand —

the Creator's Drummer, born to play

on the wonderful talking drums.